Don't Pet the Sharks

Hawaiian Coloring Book

Jupiter Kids

JUPITER KIDS
CHILDREN'S & KIDS FICTION

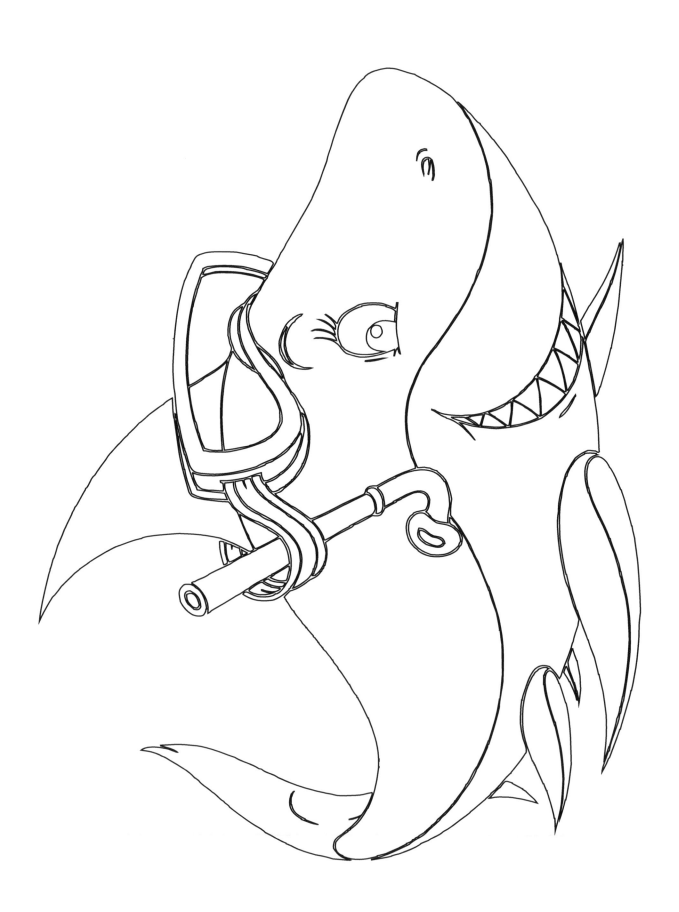

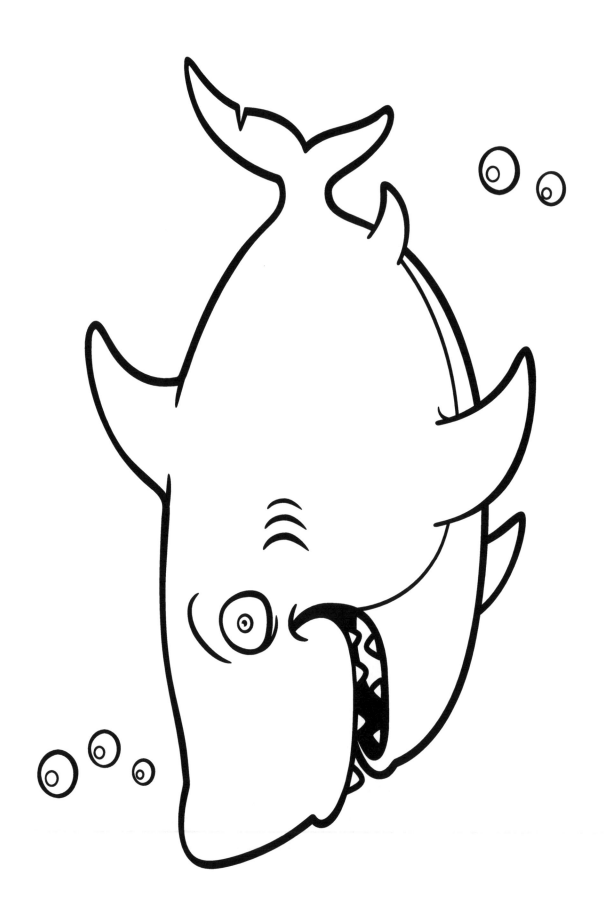

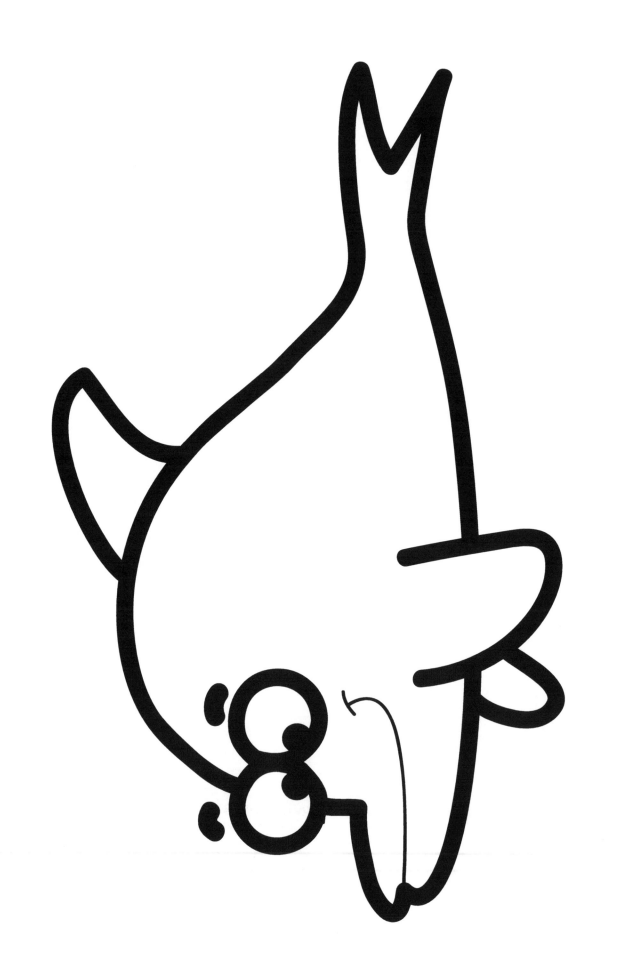

This is a Bleed Through Page If You Are Using a Coloring Marker or Pen!
Find Other Great Titles By searching for Jupiter Kids on Your Favorite Book Retailer
Amazon.Com | Barnes & Noble (BN.Com) | Books A Million (BAM.Com)

JUPITER KIDS
CHILDREN'S & KIDS FICTION

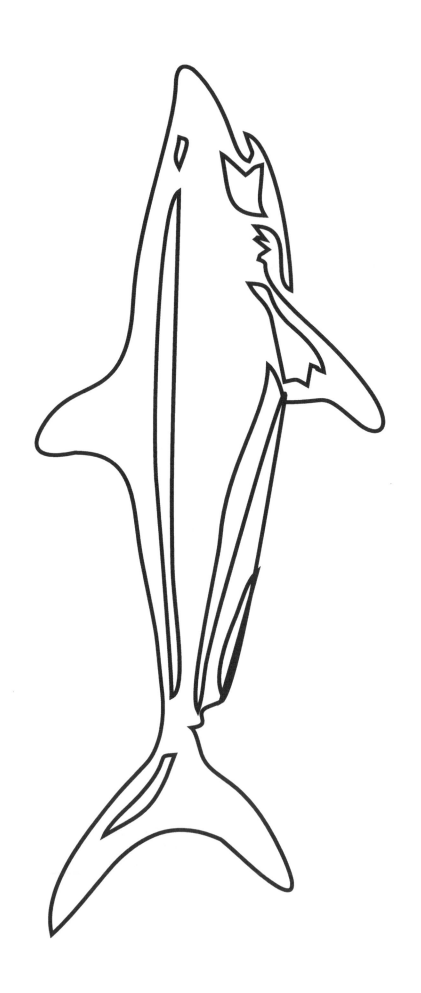

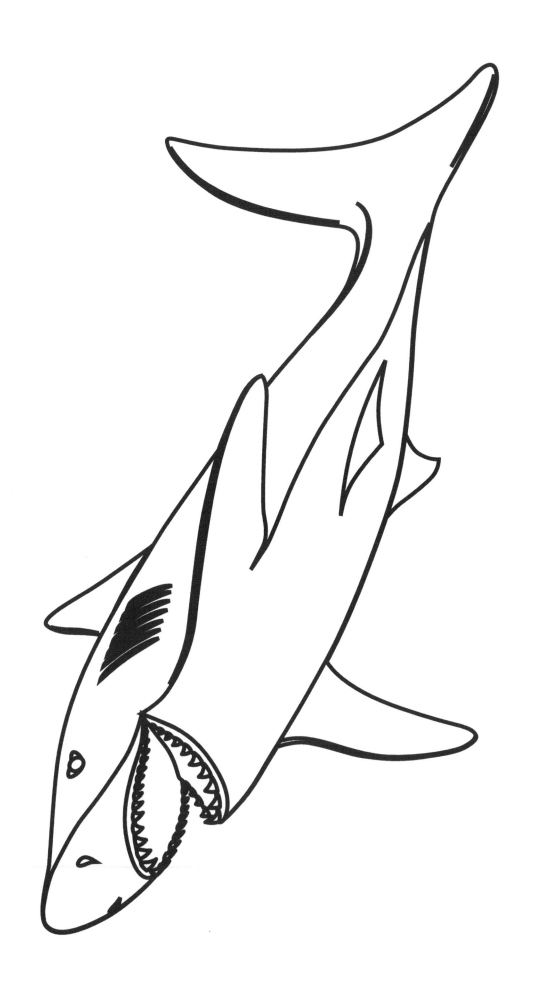

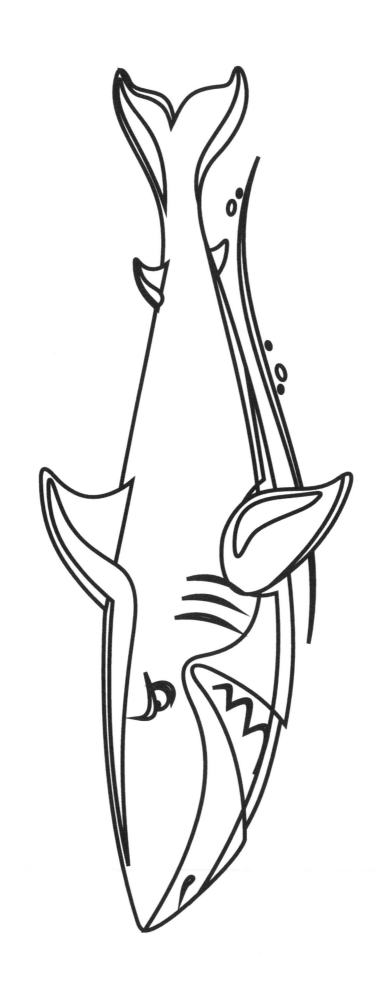

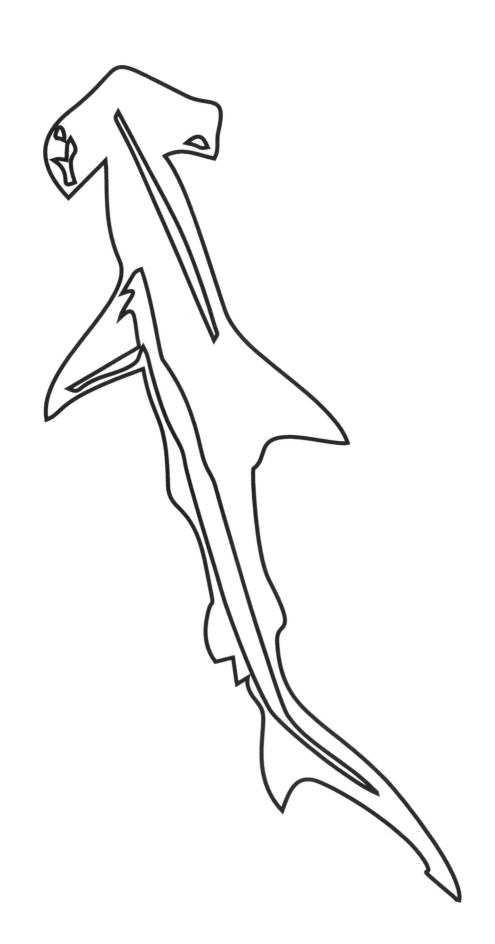

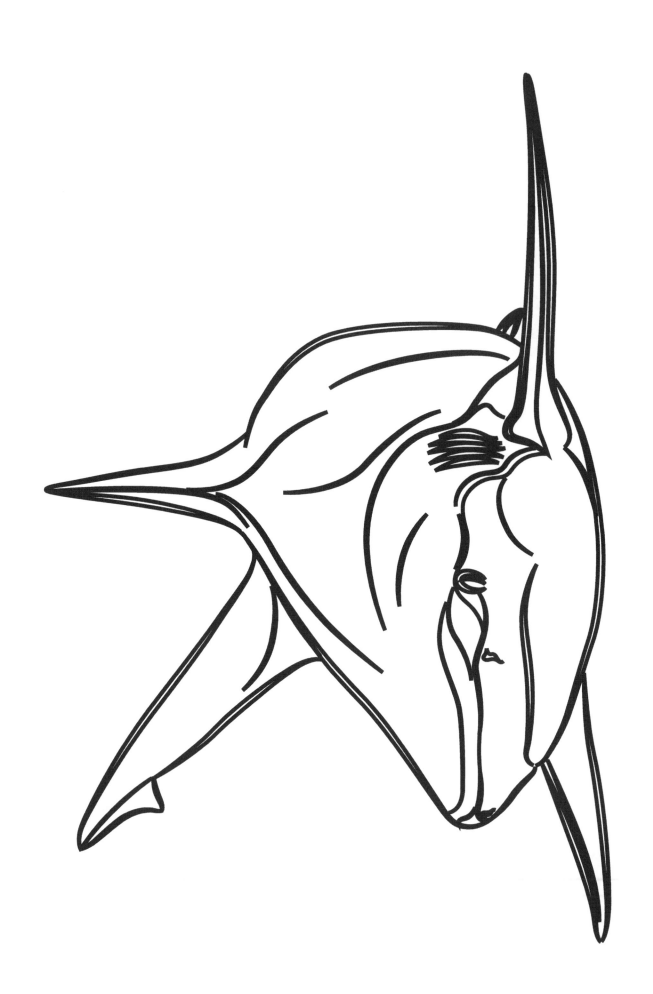